GUIDE TO THE SKY FOR SCOUTS-GUIDES

THE BHARAT SCOUTS & GUIDES PROFICIENCY BADGE COURSE WORK ON STAR MAN & STAR GAZER

ER. ARITRA DAS

Dedicated to Respected

Dr.DebiprosadDuari.

Ex-Director. M.P. Birla Planetarium

for guiding me through the stars

Contents

Preface

Please read this book as a basic guide book to observe the night sky.

Er.Aritra Das

Acknowledgements

My sincere thanks to
Mrs. Archita Chakraborty, my wife,
Ms. Rahi Nath, Amateur Astronomer,
Ms. Rohini Chatterjee, Amateur Astronomer &
Mr. Suprabhat Paul, ALT(C), Eastern Railway Bharat Scouts & Guides
for their unparalleled support

Disclaimer

I do not claim copyright of any images used in this document, all are copyrighted to their respective owners whose list may be found at the end of this handbook.

Helping Hands

1.Wikipedia

2.https://stellarium-web.org/

3.https://www.timeanddate.com/astronomy/measuring-the-sky-by-hand.html

4.https://360.here.com/2015/05/29/5-ways-to-find-north-without-a-compass

5.DuckDuckGo Searches of respective Keywords

6.http://www.webconversiononline.com/

CHAPTER ONE

Particulars as per APRO

As per APRO Part II/III

(1) Keep a log or notebook over a period of three months giving observations of Stars, Moon, and Planets (if any) visible from a window, garden or street in or near his/her own home.

Note : There should be at least one entry per week made regularly at approximately the same time in the evening.

(2) Demonstrate, with diagrams, drawings or models (preferably models), relative position and size of Sun, Moon, Earth and other planets; show their movements.

(3) Point out in the sky:

At least four constellations visible all the year round.

At least four constellations not visible all the year round.

At least four first magnitude stars; know to which constellations they belong and at what time of the year they are visible.

(4) Obtain a compass direction from the stars.

CHAPTER TWO

Particulars as in the Book

The Course is designed as per APRO coursework, but the vastness of the subject made me develop the coursework a different from normal Proficiency Badge coursework. Each point of the coursework is discussed briefly & then logbook work is described so that you can easily complete your logbook by yourself. For this purpose, the sequence of coursework is modified a little bit. You are requested to follow the sequence of APRO while preparing the logbook.

1. The Solar System: This chapter describes point no 2.
2. Measuring angular distance in the sky: This chapter is a part of point no 1.
3. Celestial Coordinate System & their alignment with the Earth: This chapter is a part of point no 1.
4. Alignment of Celestial Coordinates with ourselves: This chapter is a part of point no 1.
5. Plotting Night Sky to a paper: This chapter is a part of point no 1.
6. Equatorial Coordinate System: Declination & Right Ascension: This chapter is a part of point no 3.
7. Constellations: This chapter is a part of point no 3.

8. Compass Direction from Stars: This chapter is a part of point no 4.

CHAPTER THREE

The Solar System

The Solar System: Our night sky is full of lighted dots. Most of them are self lighted objects which are Billions of Kilometres away from us. We called them Stars (Nakshatra/ Tara in the Indian context). One of them is very close to us & we can't see it in the night sky. Almost 15 Crore Kilometre from the Earth, rises in the East & sets in the West. We called him **the Sun**, the head of our Solar System with a mass of 3.5 Lakh times more than Earth (3,33,000 × Earth).

The Sun: The Sun is the star at the centre of the Solar System. It is nearly a perfect sphere of hot plasma, heated to incandescence by Nuclear Fusion reactions in its core, radiating the energy mainly as visible light and infrared radiation. It is by far the most important source of energy for life on Earth. Its diameter is about 1.39 million kilometres (864,000 miles), or 109 times that of Earth, and its mass is about 330,000 times that of Earth. It accounts for about 99.86% of the total mass of the Solar System. Roughly three-quarters of the Sun's mass consists of Hydrogen (~73%); the rest is mostly Helium (~25%), with much smaller quantities of heavier elements, including Oxygen, Carbon, Neon, and Iron.

The family of the Sun is called the Solar System. The Solar System is the gravitationally bound system of the Sun and the objects that orbit it, either directly or indirectly. Of the objects that orbit the Sun directly, the largest are the eight planets, with the remainder being smaller objects, dwarf planets and small Solar System bodies. Of the objects that orbit the Sun indirectly—the moons—two are larger than the smallest planet, Mercury.

The above diagram shows the True size of the Planets as per scale, also you can find the distance (in scale).

The Solar System has formed 4.6 billion years ago from the gravitational collapse of a giant interstellar molecular cloud. The vast majority of the system's mass is in the Sun, with the majority of the remaining mass contained in Jupiter. The four smaller inner planets, **Mercury, Venus, Earth and Mars**, are terrestrial planets, being primarily composed of rock and metal. The four outer planets are giant planets, being substantially more massive than the terrestrials. The two largest planets, **Jupiter and Saturn**, are gas giants, being composed mainly of Hydrogen and Helium; the two outermost planets, **Uranus and Neptune**, are ice giants, being composed mostly of substances with relatively high melting points compared with Hydrogen and Helium, called volatiles, such as water, ammonia and methane. *All eight planets have almost circular orbits that lie within a nearly flat disc called the ecliptic.*

The Solar System also contains smaller objects. **The Asteroid Belt**, which lies between the orbits of Mars and Jupiter, mostly contains objects composed, like the terrestrial planets, of rock and metal. Beyond Neptune's orbit lie the **Kuiper Belt and Scattered disc**, which are populations of Trans-Neptunian objects composed mostly of ices, and beyond them a newly discovered population of sednoids. Within these populations, some objects are large enough to have rounded under their own gravity, though there is considerable debate as to how many there will prove to be. Such objects are categorized as **Dwarf Planets**. The only certain dwarf planet is **Pluto**, with another Trans-Neptunian object, **Eris**, expected to be, and the asteroid **Ceres** at least close to being a dwarf planet. In addition to these two regions, various other small-body populations, including comets, centaurs and interplanetary dust clouds, freely travel between regions. Six of the planets, the six largest possible dwarf planets, and many of the smaller bodies are orbited by natural satellites, usually termed "Moons" after the Moon. Each of the outer planets is encircled by planetary rings of dust and other small objects.

The solar wind, a stream of charged particles flowing outwards from the Sun, creates a bubble-like region in the interstellar medium known as the **Heliosphere**. The **Heliopause** is the point at which pressure from the solar wind is equal to the opposing pressure of the interstellar medium; it extends out to the edge of the Kuiper Belt. The **Oort cloud**, which is thought to be the source for long-period comets, may also exist at a distance roughly a thousand times further than the heliosphere. The Solar System is located in the **Orion Arm**, 26,000 light-years from the centre of the **Milky Way Galaxy**.

Body[note 1]	Image	Radius[note 2]		Volume		Mass		Density	Gravity[note 3]		Type	Discovery	Distance from Earth (KM)
		(km)	($R_⊕$)	(10^9 km³)	($V_⊕$)	(10^{21} kg)	($M_⊕$)	(g/cm³)	(m/s²)	(⊕)			
Sun		696 342 ±65[11]	109.3	1,414,300,000	1,305,700	1 988 500 000	333,000	1.408	274.0	27.94	star	-	14,96, 00,000
Jupiter		69 911 ±6 (w/o rings)	10.97	1,431,280	1,321	1 898 200 ±?	317.83	1.326	24.79	2.528	planet (gas giant); has rings	-	62,87, 30,000
Saturn		58 232 ±6 (w/o rings)	9.140	827,130	764	568 340 ±?	95.162	0.687	10.445	1.065	planet (gas giant); has rings	-	127,50, 00,000
Uranus		25 362 ±7	3.981	68,340	63.1	86 813 ±?	14.536	1.27	8.69	0.886	planet (ice giant); has rings	1781	272,39, 50,000
Neptune		24 622 ±19	3.865	62,540	57.7	102 413±?	17.147	1.638	11.15	1.137	planet (ice giant); has rings	1846	435,14 ,00,000
Earth		6 371.00	1	1,083.21	1	5 972.4	1	5.514	9.80665	1	planet (terrestrial)	-	
Venus		6 051.8 ±1.0 (w/o gas)	0.9499	928.43	0.857	4 867.5	0.815	5.243	8.872	0.905	planet (terrestrial)	-	4,14. 00,000
Mars		3 389.5 ±0.2	0.5320	163.18	0.151	641.7	0.107	3.9335 ± 0.0004	3.721	0.379	planet (terrestrial)	-	7,83, 40,000
Ganymede Jupiter III		2 634.1 ±0.3	0.4135	76.30	0.0704	148.2	0.0248	1.936	1.428	0.146	moon of Jupiter	1610	62,77, 66,640
Titan Saturn VI		2 574.73 ±0.09 (w/o gas)[a]	0.4037[a]	71.50	0.0658	134.5	0.0225	1.8798 ± 0.0044	1.354	0.138	moon of Saturn	1655	127,87, 00,317
Mercury		2 439.7 ±1.0	0.3829	60.83	0.0562	330.1	0.0553	5.427	3.7	0.377	planet (terrestrial)	-	9,16, 91,000
Callisto Jupiter IV		2 410.3 ±1.5	0.3783	58.65	0.0541	107.6	0.018	1.8344 ± 0.0034	1.23603	0.126	moon of Jupiter	1610	62,70, 35,570
Io Jupiter I		1 821.6 ±0.5	0.2859	25.32	0.0234	89.32	0.015	3.528 ± 0.006	1.797	0.183	moon of Jupiter	1610	62,83, 50,380
Moon (Luna) Earth I		1 737.4	0.2727	21.958	0.0203	73.42	0.0123	3.3464	1.625	0.166	moon of Earth	-	3, 84,000
Europa Jupiter II		1 560.8 ±0.5	0.2450	15.93	0.0147	48.00	0.008035	3.013 ± 0.005	1.316	0.134	moon of Jupiter	1610	62,81, 26,010
Triton Neptune I		1 353.4 ±0.9[a]	0.2124[a]	10.38	0.0096	21.39 ±0.03	0.003599	2.061	0.782	0.0797	moon of Neptune	1846	435,43, 80,680
Pluto 134340		1 188.3 ±0.8	0.187	7.057	0.00651	13.03 ±0.03	0.0022	1.854 ± 0.006	0.620	0.063	dwarf planet; plutino; multiple	1930	576,39, 20,000
Eris 136199		1 163 ±6[b][12]	0.1825[b]	6.59	0.0061	16.6 ±0.2[13]	0.0028	2.52 ±0.07	0.824	0.083	dwarf planet; SDO; binary	2003	10,12. 285,40, 73,000

The Solar System

CHAPTER FOUR

Measuring Angular Distances in the Sky

You can measure any angular distance by this method while standing on the ground.

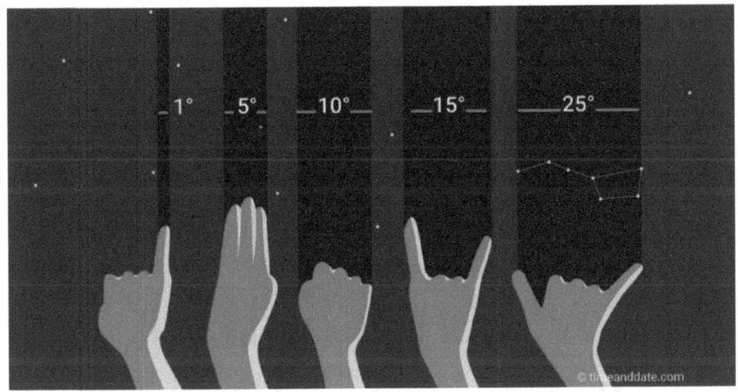

Please don't bend your elbow while making these gestures, keep your elbow straight.

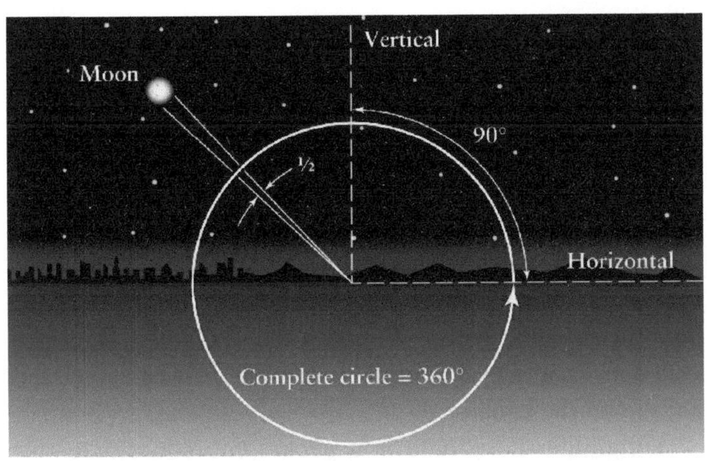

The Moon is approximately 1/2° in Night Sky.

CHAPTER FIVE

Celestial Coordinate Systems & their alignment with the Earth

The Earth is divided by Latitude & Longitude Coordinate Systems which help us to navigate & geographically locate a point on this planet.

Latitude: In geography, Latitude is a geographic coordinate that specifies the North-South position of a point on the Earth's surface, or the surface of a celestial body. Latitude is an angle that ranges from 0° at the Equator to 90° (North or South) at the poles. Lines of constant latitude, or parallels, run East-West as circles parallel to the equator.

Longitude: Longitude is a geographic coordinate that specifies the East-West position of a point on the Earth's surface, or the surface of a celestial body. It is an angular measurement, usually expressed in degrees and denoted by the Greek letter lambda (λ). Meridians (lines running from the North pole to the South pole) connect points with the same longitude. The prime meridian, which passes near the Royal Observatory, Greenwich, England, is defined as 0° longitude by convention. Positive longitudes are East of the Prime Meridian, and Negative ones are West.

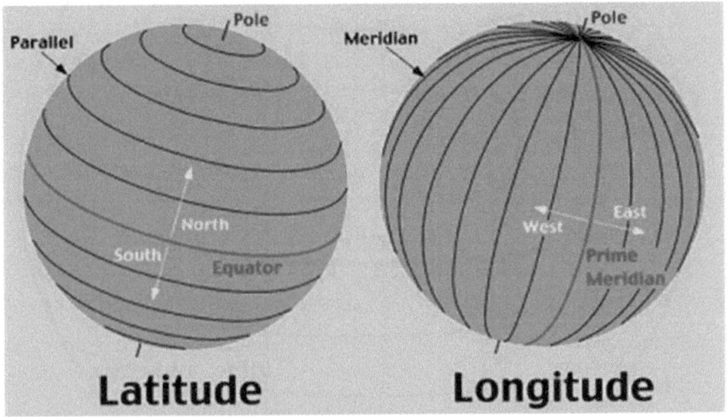

Latitude & Longitude

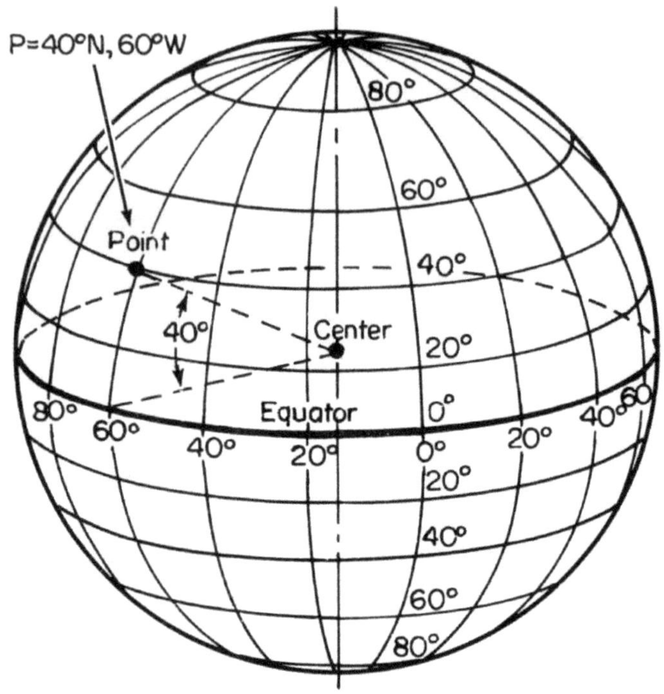

Latitude & Longitude

North Pole: In this course, North means True North, which is indicated by Polaris/ Pole Star/ Dhruba Tara (in the Indian context) which is the name of the brightest star in the constellation Ursa Minor (that's why it is called Alpha Ursae Minoris).

If you are standing at the North Pole, i.e. exactly 90°N, then you will find the Pole Star in the Zenith Point.

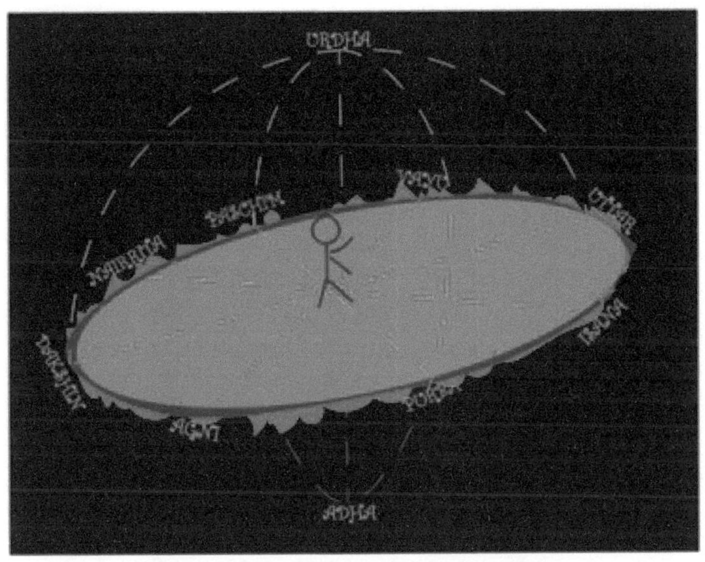

Along with 4 Cardinal Points (North East West South) & 4 half cardinal points (North-East, South-East, South-West & North-West), which denote the 2-dimensional surfaces of the Earth we need another dimension in the Up-Down direction to plot the Sky, which is an eventually 3-dimensional surface. Upward Point is called Zenith (Urdha in the Indian context) & Downward Point is called Nadir (Adha in the Indian context). Actually, Adha always points to the centre of the Earth.

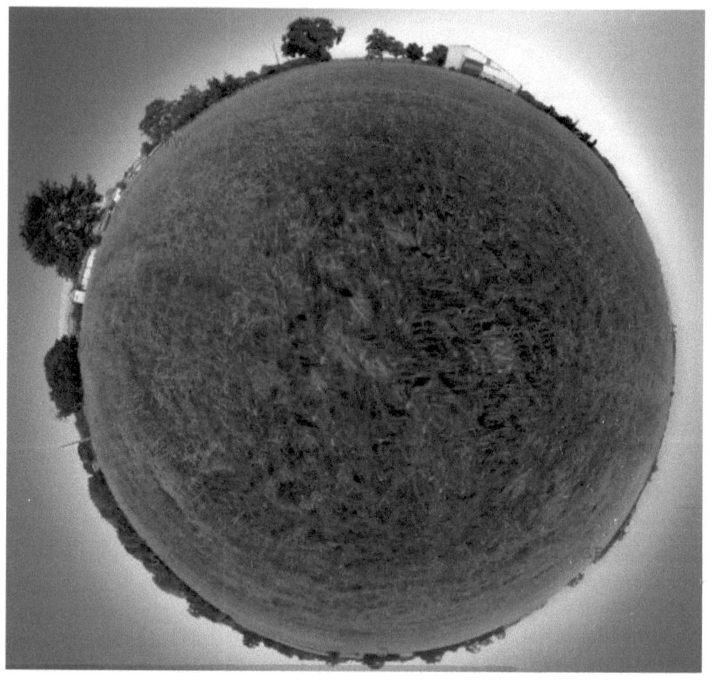

Cardinal & Half -Cardinal Points: We have divided our Horizon into 4 Cardinal Points & 4 Half Cardinal Points. Those points are marked at Horizon.

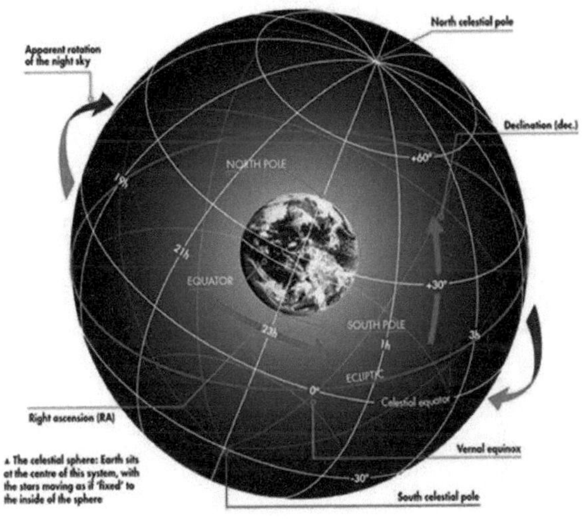

▲ The celestial sphere: Earth sits at the centre of this system, with the stars moving as if 'fixed' to the inside of the sphere

Celestial Coordinates: If we extend our Latitude & Longitude lines towards the universe up to our visibility, we will create the same coordinate system in the sky. The boundary of that visibility limit will create an imaginary Sphere which is called the Celestial Sphere. We can imagine that everything which we see at the Sky at any point in time is projected at the **Celestial Sphere.**

Our Equator becomes the Celestial Equator, Our North Pole becomes Celestial North Pole & Our South pole becomes Celestial South Pole in that Celestial Sphere.

CHAPTER SIX

Alignment of Celestial Coordinates with ourselves

The Sky changes with respect to the place where the observer is standing, Thus it is important to know how the sky will change with respect to places. Generally, a star's true position remains the same for an observer throughout his lifetime, but due to the Earth's rotation around the Sun & its own axis changes the Sky.

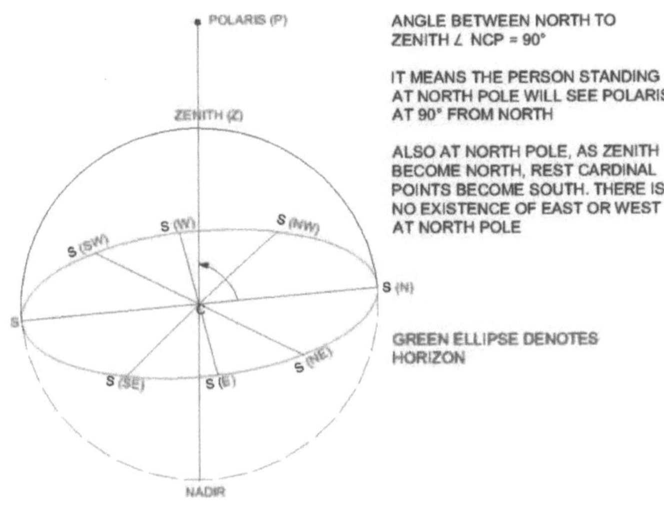
POLARIS (P)
ANGLE BETWEEN NORTH TO ZENITH ∠ NCP = 90°
IT MEANS THE PERSON STANDING AT NORTH POLE WILL SEE POLARIS AT 90° FROM NORTH
ALSO AT NORTH POLE, AS ZENITH BECOME NORTH, REST CARDINAL POINTS BECOME SOUTH. THERE IS NO EXISTENCE OF EAST OR WEST AT NORTH POLE
ZENITH (Z)
S (W)
S (NW)
S (SW)
S (N)
S
C
GREEN ELLIPSE DENOTES HORIZON
S (SE)
S (E)
S (NE)
NADIR

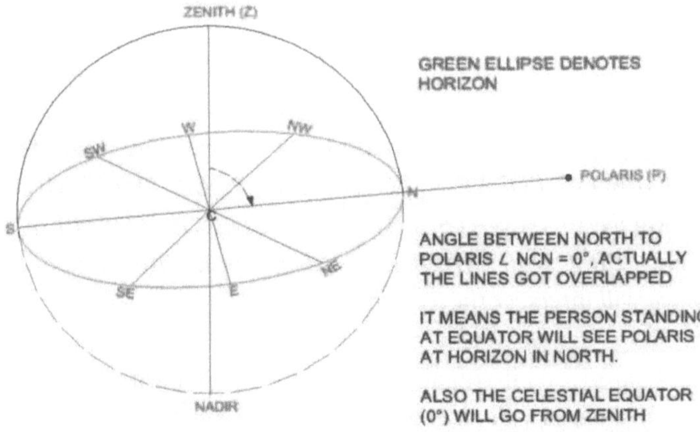
ZENITH (Z)
GREEN ELLIPSE DENOTES HORIZON
W
NW
SW
POLARIS (P)
N
S
C
ANGLE BETWEEN NORTH TO POLARIS ∠ NCN = 0°, ACTUALLY THE LINES GOT OVERLAPPED
NE
SE
E
IT MEANS THE PERSON STANDING AT EQUATOR WILL SEE POLARIS AT HORIZON IN NORTH.
ALSO THE CELESTIAL EQUATOR (0°) WILL GO FROM ZENITH
NADIR

Also, the person who is standing at the Equator will see Polaris at Horizon.

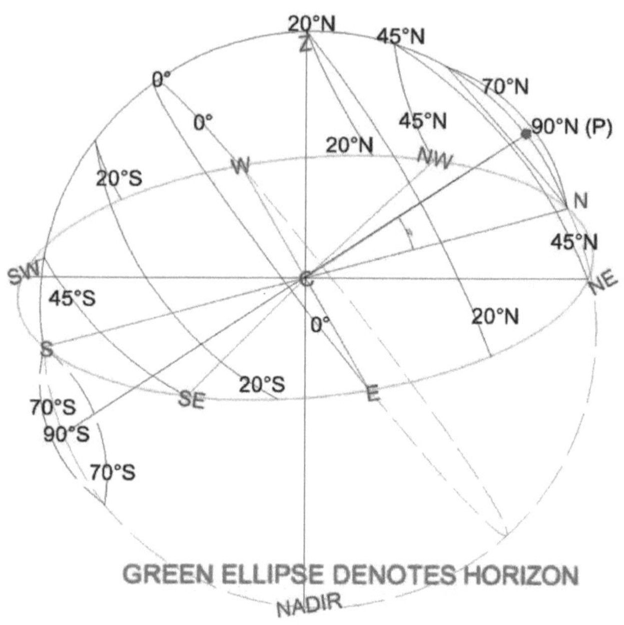

So, from the above diagrams, we can say that *THE ANGLE OF POLARIS TO NORTH POLE THROUGH A PERSON IS ALWAYS THE LATITUDE OF THE PLACE, THE PERSON IS STANDING. Also, The Latitude line of the place will intersect the Zenith Point.*

<u>That means if you are standing at 20°N Latitude:</u>

the Polaris will rise 20° from the North (∠ NCP = 20°) direction towards Zenith,

•the 20°N Celestial Latitude line will intersect your Zenith Point.

•the 70°N Celestial Latitude line will always remain visible to you at any point in time. Because Zenith to Horizon is 90° & rise of the Polaris is 20°, the (90°-20°)=70° circle will always remain visible.

•Stars & constellations that are situated at 70°N to 90°N Celestial Latitudes will remain visible to you at any point in time.

•the 70°S Celestial Latitude line will always remain invisible to you at any point in time.

•Stars & Constellations which are situated at 70°S to 90°S Celestial Latitude will remain invisible to you at any point in time.

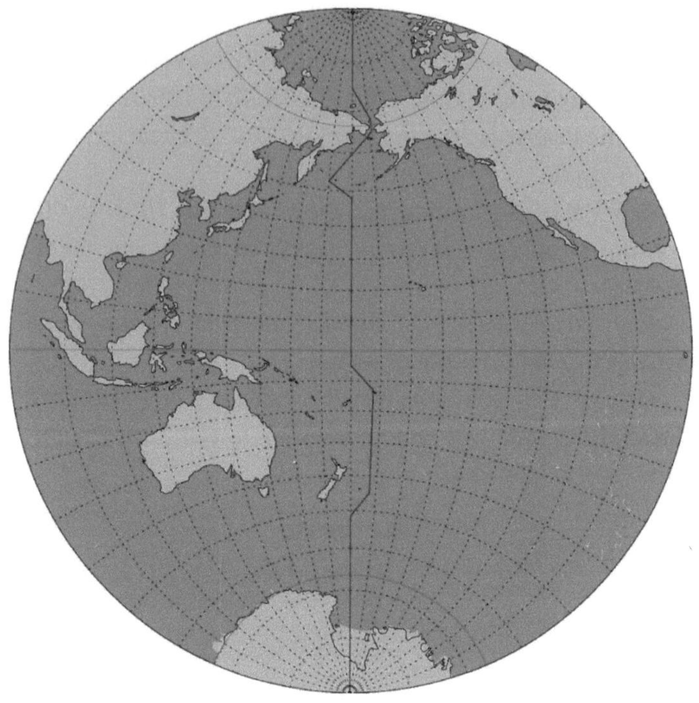

Longitude Lines are different in Astronomy. In Geography Longitude lines are drawn by dividing the Equator into 24 equal parts & drawing North Pole South Pole connectors through them. Each line resembles 1 hour. The Sun passes through each one of them Every day. In 1984 an International conference defines that the Longitude passes through Greenwich, England will be in the middle of that line. So, the Longitude of Greenwich is Zero, or we can say Greenwich is Prime Meridian Eastward lines will bear positive (+ve) degree line (0 to +180), Westward will bear (-ve) degree line (0 to -180). As Earth is a sphere, +180 & -180 also meet in a single line, We called it International Date Line.

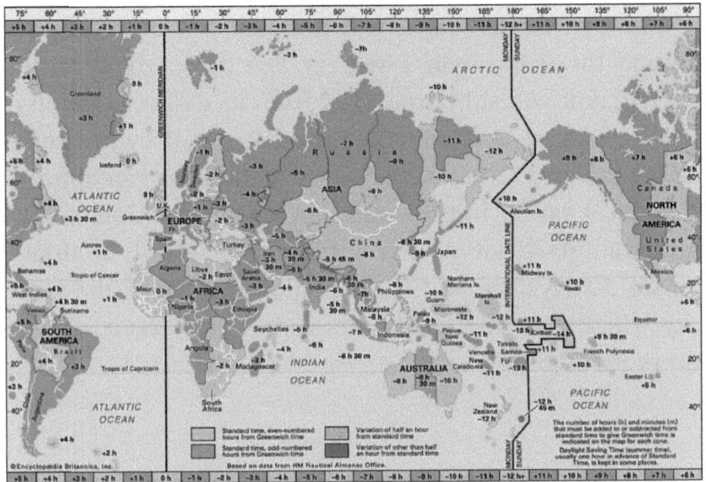

If you are standing at the Equator in Prime Meridian (i.e. 0° N/S) at 12 Noon on 1st January in any year, then you will find the Sun exactly at your Zenith)

In Astronomy, we renamed those Latitude degrees as Hours, Minutes, and Seconds.

360 lines resemble 24 hours. This means 1 Hour line resembles 15 degrees, or 1° equal to 4 Minutes.

As the Earth rotates 1 revolution around the Sun in exactly 1 year, we will see the exact Sky Map for a particular date & time exactly after 1 Year. This means the star chart you made on 1st January 2020 at 7 PM from your home location, the Same star chart will repeat on 1st January 2021, at 7 PM from your home location, the only difference is that the Position of Moon & Planets will be changed. But the position of stars will not be changed.

There is another significance of this thing.

For a particular star it will complete a 360° revolution around the Polestar in 1 year or 365 days, which means every day it will shift around 1° from its earlier position if you are looking at it from the same location. Now we know 1° *is* equal to 4 Minutes, so every day the same star appears 4 minutes earlier in the same spot if your position of sky-observation is not changed. In another word, a Month means 30 days, so 30*4=120 minutes or 2 hours, the same sky will appear almost 2 hours early on the same date of every month.

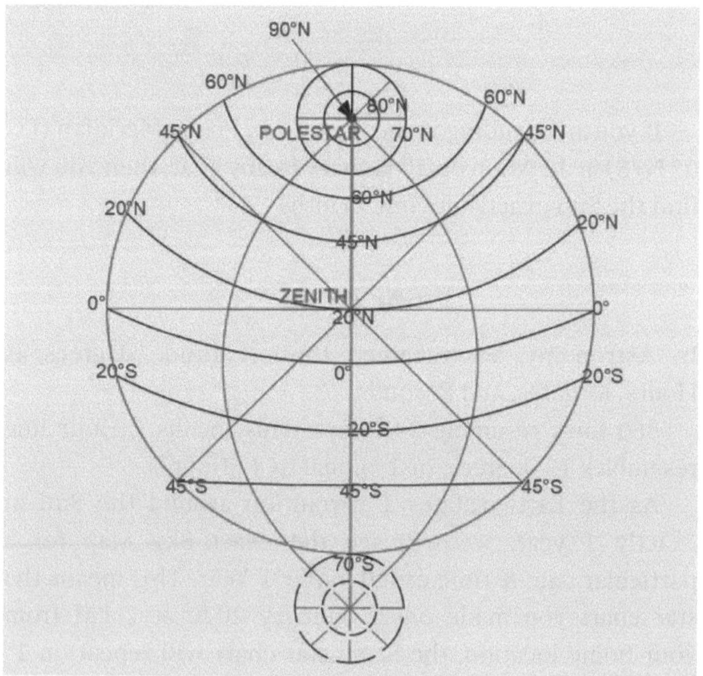

If you join the Polestar & Zenith point & extends it in both North-South directions, the generated Line will resemble the Longitude line. It means at any point of our day one Longitude line is always directly over our head.

CHAPTER SEVEN

Plotting Night Sky to a paper

Remember that plotting a 3 Dimensional surface to a 2 Dimensional plane is a tough thing & also requires practice & imagination.

When we map an Earth's Surface facing North, then we draw the map as it is just beneath our foot. This means we are facing the ground. Thus our Right hand denotes East & Left hand denotes West.

But when we are mapping the Sky, we are actually facing towards the sky, like we are sleeping on the roof with our head in the North & leg in the South direction & gazing at the sky. At that moment the East-West Direction got changed. Then our left hand denotes East & Right hand is denoting West.

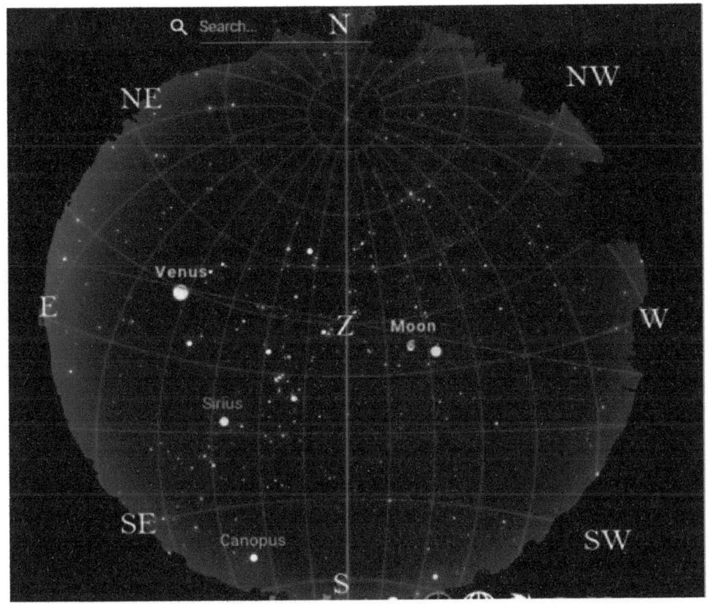

The above pic is taken from 22°N latitude, thus 22°N Celestial Latitude is intersecting the North-South line at point Z(Zenith).

So, when we see a Star we measure its angular distance from the horizon & its bearing from either a compass or from hand measurements at a horizontal level & plot that star to the below Star chart.

<u>The Star Chart:</u>

•Locate the True North on the Horizon by any means.

•Select the star you want to plot. Name it "T"

•Draw an imaginary line from Zenith to the star & extend the line towards its nearest Horizon. Mark the point (H) visually by any non movable object like trees, buildings, etc. Let's give the imaginary line an Imaginary name “ZH”.

•Take the angular distance of that point at Horizon (H) from North clockwise (towards East). You can use a Compass or can take hand gestures. Write it as “NH”.

•Measure the angular distance of the star (T) from that point at the horizon (H) in the ZH line. Write the distance as “TH”.

•Convert the angle which we got from TH° as THp mm per the table mentioned.

•Keep the angle that we got from NH as an angle.

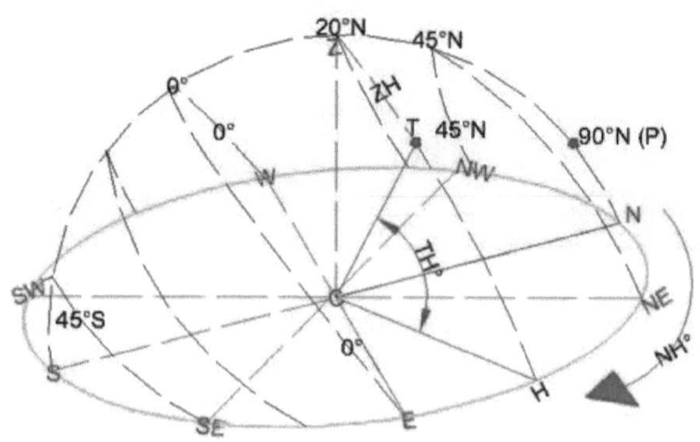

THE 3 DIMENSIONAL SKY

Sl No	Object Type (Star/ Planet)	If Identified then write the name	Angle of Object from North at Horizon (NH°)	Angle of the Object from Horizon at Zenith Horizon Line (TH°)	Convert TH° = THp mm as per side table	Conversion Table			
1						5°	8 mm	50°	57 mm
2						10°	15 mm	55°	62 (61.5) mm
3						15°	21 mm	60°	66 mm
4						20°	27 mm	65°	70 mm
5						25°	33 mm	70°	74 mm
6						30°	38 mm	75°	78 mm
7						35°	43 mm	80°	82 mm
8						40°	48 mm	85°	86 mm
9						45°	53 (52.5) mm	90°	90 mm
10									

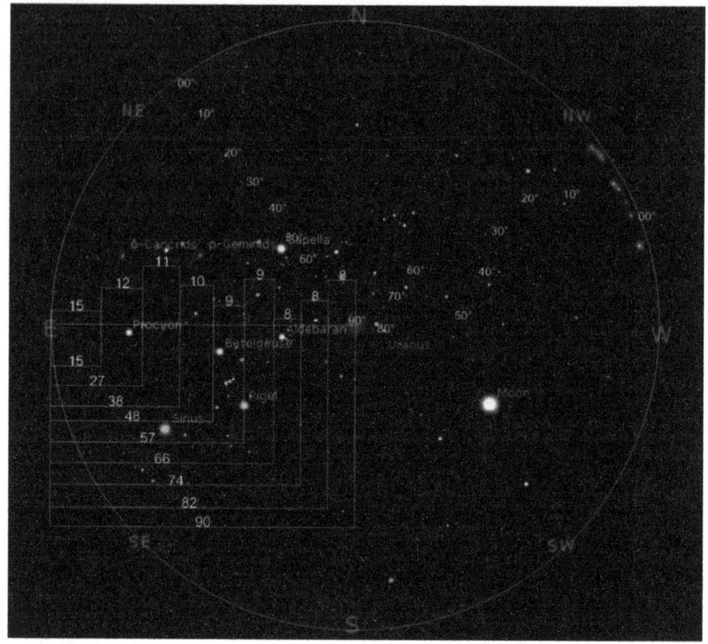

When you are viewing the sky from laying on the ground you will not experience it as a semi-sphere due to our perspective vision. Rather you will experience it like a distorted sphere whose top part is a bit flattened. Thus the Latitude circles will not evenly be distributed throughout the celestial Sphere.

SL No	Angle of Object from North at Horizon (NH°) Latitude Circle	Distance in mm from Horizon circle in 2D (where 90° = 90mm)	Difference between two consecutive angles (2D) in mm	% Distance covered from Horizon (This scale may be used for personalised Sky maps)
1	0°	0		0
2	5°	8	8	9
3	10°	15	7	17
4	15°	21	6	23
5	20°	27	6	30
6	25°	33	6	37
7	30°	38	5	42
8	35°	43	5	48
9	40°	48	5	53
10	45°	52.5	4.5	58
11	50°	57	4.5	63
12	55°	61.5	4.5	68
13	60°	66	4.5	73
14	65°	70	4	78
15	70°	74	4	82
16	75°	78	4	87
17	80°	82	4	91
18	85°	86	4	96
19	90°	90	4	100

The Latitude Circles will be distributed as per the following table.

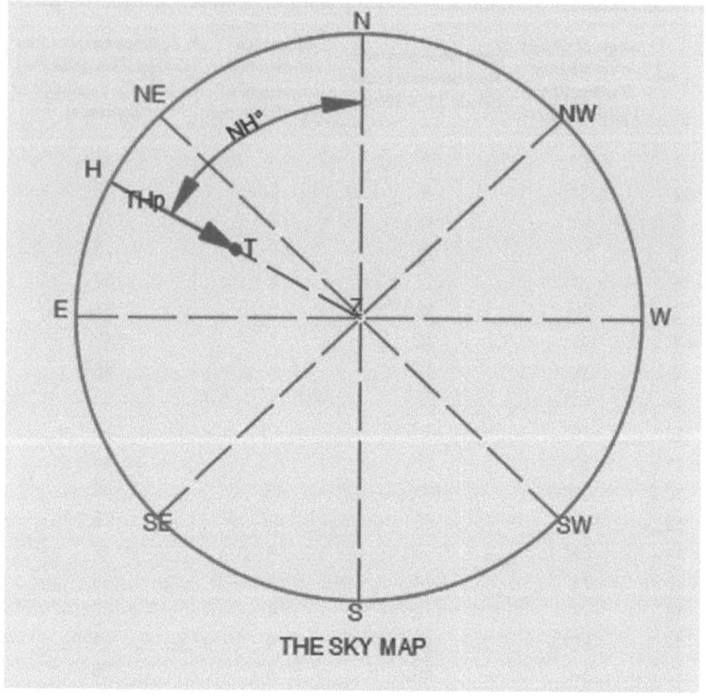

THE SKY MAP

•Now Plot this to the Skymap as shown in the figure.

•Draw a circle in your logbook with a radius of 9 cm (90mm), so the diameter will become 18 cm (180 mm) & 00° to 90° in latitude lines will be 90 mm. Draw Cardinal & Half-Cardinal points that are 45° apart from each other. Name the center Z(Zenith).

After you have completed your sky map, put it above your head & align it with North. You will see that the East point of your Map (which was at your left while drawing) is now automatically aligned with the actual East.

You will find the blank format of the Sky map at the end of the book which will be required to keep the log. In the sky condition column please write if the sky was Absolutely Clear/ Clear/ Fog/ Cloudy/Rainy.

As per APRO keep a record of the sky at approx. same time, at least once a week over a period of three months. I have attached 2 such hand-drawn maps for your reference only.

CHAPTER EIGHT

Equatorial Coordinate System: Declination & Right Ascension

Declination

The Declination symbol δ, (lower case "delta", abbreviated DEC) measures the angular distance of an object perpendicular to the Celestial Equator, positive to the North, negative to the South. For example, the North Celestial Pole has a declination of +90°. The origin of Declination is the Celestial Equator, which is the projection of the Earth's Equator onto the Celestial Sphere. Declination is analogous to terrestrial Latitude.

Right Ascension

The Right Ascension symbol α, (lower case "alpha", abbreviated RA) measures the angular distance of an object eastward along the Celestial Equator from the Vernal Equinox to the hour circle passing through the object. The Vernal Equinox point is one of the two where the Ecliptic intersects the Celestial Equator. Analogous to terrestrial longitude, Right Ascension is usually measured in sidereal hours, minutes, and seconds instead of degrees, a result of the method of measuring Right Ascensions by timing the passage of objects across the Meridian as the Earth rotates. There are 360°/24h = 15° in one hour of Right Ascension, and 24h of Right Ascension around the entire Celestial Equator.

When used together, Right Ascension and Declination are usually abbreviated as RA/Dec.

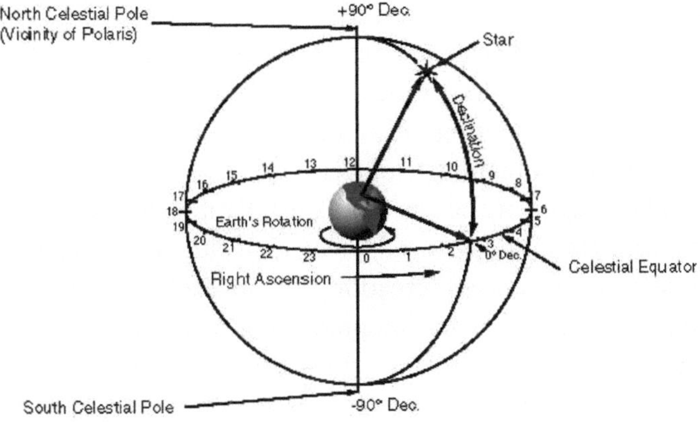

CHAPTER NINE

Constellations

A **Constellation** is an area on the Celestial Sphere in which a group of visible stars forms a perceived outline or pattern, typically representing an animal, mythological person or creature, or an inanimate object.

The origins of the earliest Constellations likely go back to prehistory. People used them to relate stories of their beliefs, experiences, creation, or mythology. Different cultures and countries adopted their own constellations, some of which lasted into the early 20th century before today's constellations were internationally recognized. The recognition of constellations has changed significantly over time. Many have changed in size or shape. Some became popular, only to drop into obscurity. Others were limited to a single culture or nation.

The 48 traditional Western constellations are Greek. They are given in Aratus' work *Phenomena* and Ptolemy's *Almagest*, though their origin probably predates these works by several centuries. Constellations in the far southern sky were added from the 15th century until the mid-18th century when European explorers began traveling to the Southern Hemisphere. Twelve ancient constellations belong to the Zodiac (straddling the Ecliptic, which the Sun, Moon, and Planets all traverse). The origins of the zodiac remain historically uncertain; its astrological divisions became prominent c. 400 BC in Babylonian or Chaldean astronomy.

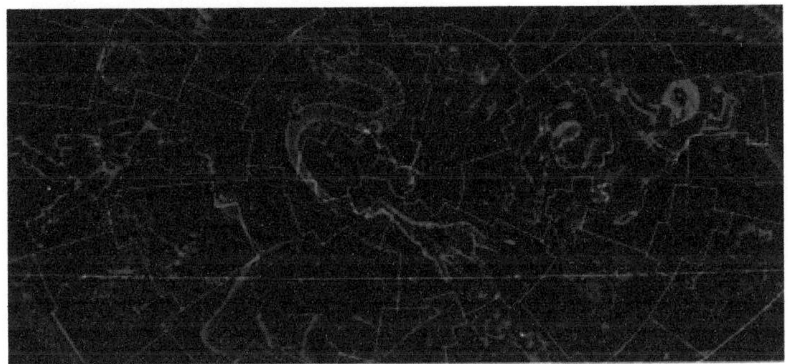

In 1922, the International Astronomical Union (IAU) formally accepted the modern list of 88 constellations, and in 1928 adopted official constellation boundaries that together cover the entire celestial sphere. Any given point in a celestial coordinate system lies in one of the modern constellations. Some astronomical naming systems include the constellation where a given celestial object is found to convey its approximate location in the sky. The Flamsteed designation of a star, for example, consists of a number and the genitive form of the constellation name.

If observed through the year, the Constellations shift gradually to the West. This is caused by the Earth's orbit around our Sun. In the summer, viewers are looking in a different direction in space at night than they are during the winter.

Other star patterns or groups called Asterisms are not Constellations but are used by observers to navigate the night sky. Asterisms may be several stars within a constellation, or they may share stars with more than one Constellation. Examples of Asterisms include the teapot in Sagittarius, the Big dipper in Ursa Major, the Summer triangle between Vega (Lyra), Deneb (Cygnus) & Altair (Aquila), and the False Cross split between the southern constellations Carina and Vela.

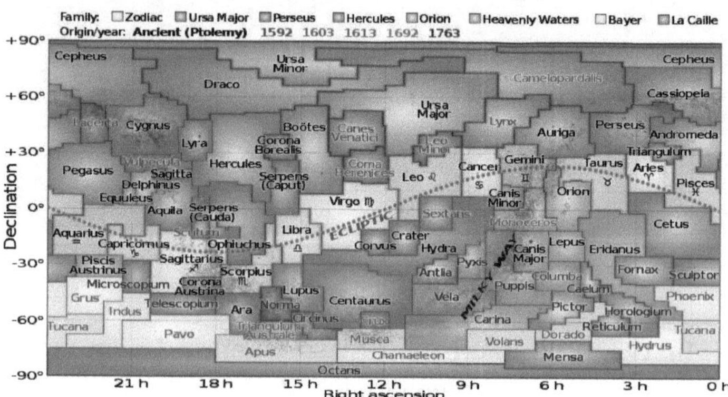

If you project the celestial sphere along with all 88 Constellations in Mercator projection the Celestial sphere will look like this. 90 N 90S, the 2 points will be drawn like a line on the top & bottom of the paper. Equator & Prime Meridian will go through from the middle of the page & intersect with each other. All Longitude lines will go vertically parallel to each other. Ecliptic is the line of the passing of the Sun through Celestial Coordinate.

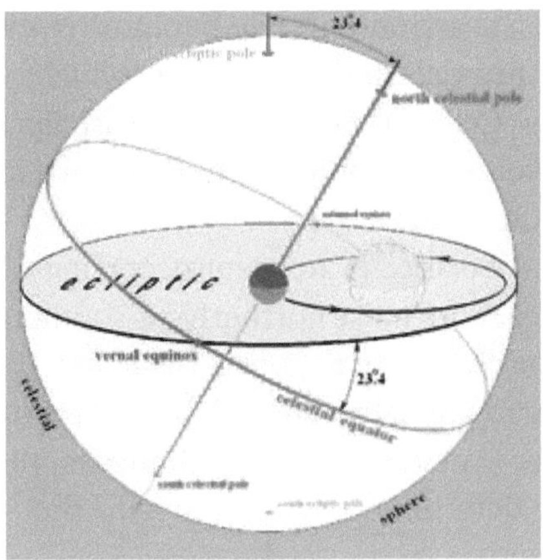

The ecliptic is the plane of Earth's orbit around the Sun. From the perspective of an observer on Earth, the Sun's movement around the celestial sphere over the course of a year traces out a path along the ecliptic against the background of stars.

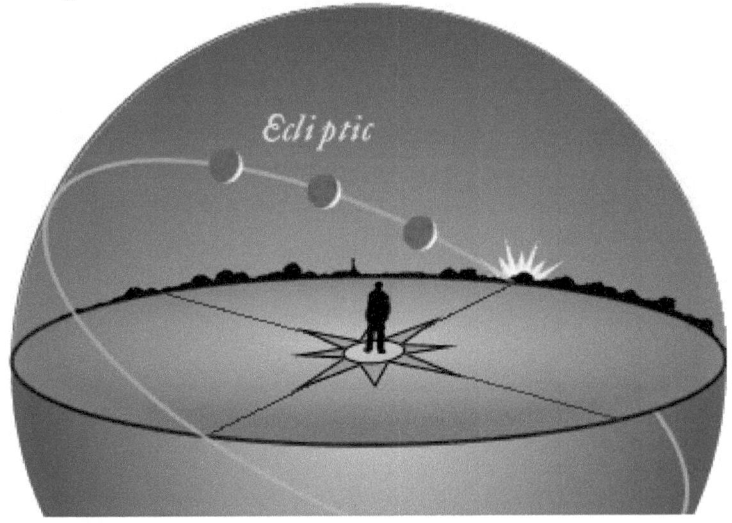

Equinox: In astronomy, an Equinox is either of two places on the Celestial Sphere at which the Ecliptic intersects the Celestial Equator. Those are Spring (Vernal) Equinox & Autumnal Equinox. On these two days, the Day & Night becomes Equal.

Solstice: A Solstice is an event occurring when the Sun appears to reach its most northerly or southerly excursion relative to the celestial equator on the celestial sphere. Two solstices occur annually, around June 21 (Summer) and December 21 (Winter). In many countries, the seasons of the year are determined by reference to the Solstices and the Equinoxes.

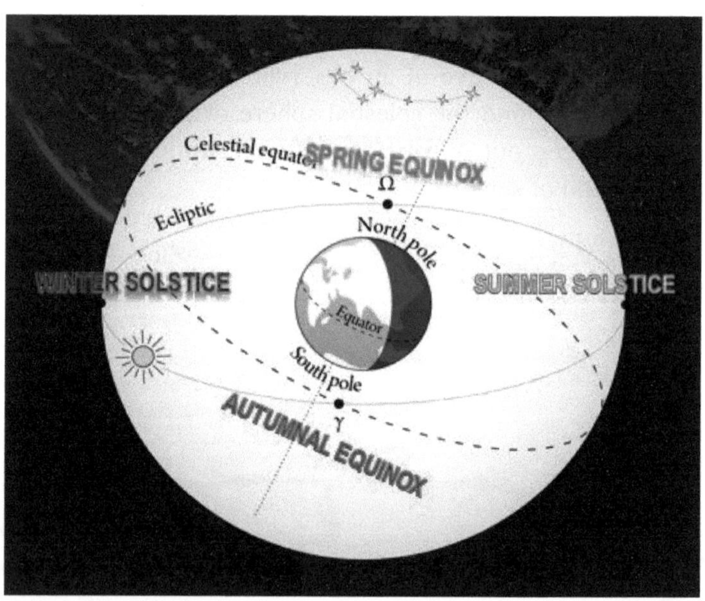

Rank	Abbrev.	Constellation	% Area covered in sky	Right Ascension (Hr Min Sec)	Decli-nation (Degs & mins)
1	Hya	Hydra	3.16%	+11 36.73	−14 31.91
2	Vir	Virgo	3.14%	+13 24.39	−04 09.51
3	UMa	Ursa Major	3.10%	+11 18.76	+50 43.27
4	Cet	Cetus	2.99%	+01 40.10	−07 10.76
5	Her	Hercules	2.97%	+17 23.16	+27 29.93
6	Eri	Eridanus	2.76%	+03 18.02	−28 45.37
7	Peg	Pegasus	2.72%	+22 41.84	+19 27.98
8	Dra	Draco	2.63%	+15 08.64	+67 00.40
9	Cen	Centaurus	2.57%	+13 04.27	−47 20.72
10	Aqr	Aquarius	2.38%	+22 17.38	−10 47.35
11	Oph	Ophiuchus	2.30%	+17 23.69	−07 54.74
12	Leo	Leo	2.30%	+10 40.03	+13 08.32
13	Boo	Boötes	2.20%	+14 42.64	+31 12.16
14	Psc	Pisces	2.16%	+00 28.97	+13 41.23
15	Sgr	Sagittarius	2.10%	+19 05.94	−28 28.61
16	Cyg	Cygnus	1.95%	+20 35.28	+44 32.70
17	Tau	Taurus	1.93%	+04 42.13	+14 52.63
18	Cam	Camelopardalis	1.83%	+08 51.37	+69 22.89
19	And	Andromeda	1.75%	+00 48.46	+37 25.91
20	Pup	Puppis	1.63%	+07 15.48	−31 10.64
21	Aur	Auriga	1.59%	+06 04.42	+42 01.68
22	Aql	Aquila	1.58%	+19 40.02	+03 24.65

Rank	Abbrev.	Constellation	% Area covered in sky	Right Ascension (Hr Min Sec)	Decli-nation (Degs & mins)
23	Ser	Serpens	1.54%	+16 57.04	+06 07.32
24	Per	Perseus	1.49%	+03 10.50	+45 00.79
25	Cas	Cassiopeia	1.45%	+01 19.16	+62 11.04
26	Ori	Orion	1.44%	+05 34.59	+05 56.94
27	Cep	Cepheus	1.42%	+02 32.64	+71 00.51
28	Lyn	Lynx	1.32%	+07 59.53	+47 28.00
29	Lib	Libra	1.30%	+15 11.96	-15 14.08
30	Gem	Gemini	1.25%	+07 04.24	+22 36.01
31	Cnc	Cancer	1.23%	+08 38.96	+19 48.35
32	Vel	Vela	1.21%	+09 34.64	-47 10.03
33	Sco	Scorpius	1.20%	+16 53.24	-27 01.89
34	Car	Carina	1.20%	+08 41.70	-63 13.16
35	Mon	Monoceros	1.17%	+07 03.63	+00 16.93
36	Scl	Sculptor	1.15%	+00 26.28	-32 05.30
37	Phe	Phoenix	1.14%	+00 55.91	-48 34.84
38	CVn	Canes Venatici	1.13%	+13 06.96	+40 06.11
39	Ari	Aries	1.07%	+02 38.16	+20 47.54
40	Cap	Capricornus	1.00%	+21 02.93	-18 01.39
41	For	Fornax	0.96%	+02 47.88	-31 38.07
42	Com	Coma Berenices	0.94%	+12 47.27	+23 18.34
43	CMa	Canis Major	0.92%	+06 49.74	-22 08.42
44	Pav	Pavo	0.92%	+19 36.71	-65 46.89

Rank	Abbrev.	Constellation	% Area covered in sky	Right Ascension (Hr Min Sec)	Decli-nation (Degs & mins)
45	Gru	Grus	0.89%	+22 27.39	-46 21.11
46	Lup	Lupus	0.81%	+15 13.21	-42 42.53
47	Sex	Sextans	0.76%	+10 16.29	-02 36.88
48	Tuc	Tucana	0.71%	+23 46.64	-65 49.80
49	Ind	Indus	0.71%	+21 58.33	-59 42.40
50	Oct	Octans	0.71%	+23 00.00	-82 09.12
51	Lep	Lepus	0.70%	+05 33.95	-19 02.78
52	Lyr	Lyra	0.69%	+18 51.17	+36 41.36
53	Crt	Crater	0.68%	+11 23.75	-15 55.74
54	Col	Columba	0.65%	+05 51.76	-35 05.67
55	Vul	Vulpecula	0.65%	+20 13.88	+24 26.56
56	UMi	Ursa Minor	0.62%	+15 00.00	+77 41.99
57	Tel	Telescopium	0.61%	+19 19.54	-51 02.21
58	Hor	Horologium	0.60%	+03 16.56	-53 20.18
59	Pic	Pictor	0.60%	+05 42.46	-53 28.45
60	PsA	Piscis Austrinus	0.59%	+22 17.07	-30 38.53
61	Hyi	Hydrus	0.59%	+02 20.65	-69 57.39
62	Ant	Antlia	0.58%	+10 16.43	-32 29.01
63	Ara	Ara	0.57%	+17 22.49	-56 35.30
64	LMi	Leo Minor	0.56%	+10 14.72	+32 08.08
65	Pyx	Pyxis	0.54%	+08 57.16	-27 21.10
66	Mic	Microscopium	0.51%	+20 57.88	-36 16.49

Rank	Abbrev.	Constellation	% Area covered in sky	Right Ascension (Hr Min Sec)	Decli-nation (Degs & mins)
67	Aps	Apus	0.50%	+16 08.65	-75 18.00
68	Lac	Lacerta	0.49%	+22 27.68	+46 02.51
69	Del	Delphinus	0.46%	+20 41.61	+11 40.26
70	Crv	Corvus	0.45%	+12 26.52	-18 26.20
71	CMi	Canis Minor	0.44%	+07 39.17	+06 25.63
72	Dor	Dorado	0.43%	+05 14.51	-59 23.22
73	CrB	Corona Borealis	0.43%	+15 50.59	+32 37.49
74	Nor	Norma	0.40%	+15 54.18	-51 21.09
75	Men	Mensa	0.37%	+05 24.90	-77 30.24
76	Vol	Volans	0.34%	+07 47.73	-69 48.07
77	Mus	Musca	0.34%	+12 35.28	-70 09.66
78	Tri	Triangulum	0.32%	+02 11.07	+31 28.56
79	Cha	Chamaeleon	0.32%	+10 41.53	-79 12.30
80	CrA	Corona Australis	0.31%	+18 38.79	-41 08.85
81	Cae	Caelum	0.30%	+04 42.27	-37 52.90
82	Ret	Reticulum	0.28%	+03 55.27	-59 59.85
83	TrA	Triangulum Australe	0.27%	+16 04.95	-65 23.28
84	Sct	Scutum	0.26%	+18 40.39	-09 53.32
85	Cir	Circinus	0.23%	+14 34.54	-63 01.82
86	Sge	Sagitta	0.19%	+19 39.05	+18 51.68
87	Equ	Equuleus	0.17%	+21 11.26	+07 45.49
88	Cru	Crux	0.17%	+12 26.99	-60 11.19

For Question no 3, We have to find out which constellations we are required to know.

<u>At least four Constellations are visible all the year-round.</u>

Only Circumpolar Constellations are either visible all year round or they will never be visible from a place. It means if you are standing at 20° *N*, then the constellation that is inside of 70°N to 90°*N* Celestial coordinates are only visible throughout the year because they will never set below the horizon. Also, You can never able to see

70 °S to 90 °S constellations. Remember, there are no such constellations if you are at the Equator.

The latitude of the Mainland of India lies between 6° 44′°N to 35° 30′°N, so the following Constellations may be called circumpolar as per the Indian context.

1.Ursa Major
2.Ursa Minor
3.Cepheus
4.Cassiopeia

<u>At least four constellations are not visible all year round.</u>

They are called Seasonal Constellations. All who are not circumpolar are seasonal.

The following constellations are prominent circumpolar as per the Indian context.

1.Orion
2.Cygnus
3.Lyra
4.Bootes

<u>At least four first magnitude stars; know to which constellations they belong and at what time of the year they are visible.</u>

In astronomy, Magnitude is a unitless measure of the brightness of an object in a defined passband, often in the visible or infrared spectrum, but sometimes across all wavelengths. An imprecise but systematic determination of the magnitude of objects was introduced in ancient times by Hipparchus.

The scale is logarithmic and defined such that each step of one magnitude changes the brightness by a factor of the fifth root of 100, or approximately 2.512. For example, a magnitude 1 star is exactly 100 times brighter than a magnitude 6 star. The brighter an object appears, the lower the value of its magnitude, with the brightest objects reaching negative values.

Astronomers use two different definitions of magnitude: apparent magnitude and absolute magnitude. The apparent magnitude (m) is the brightness of an object as it appears in the night sky from Earth. Apparent magnitude depends on an object's intrinsic luminosity, its distance, and the extinction reducing its brightness. The absolute magnitude (M) describes the intrinsic luminosity emitted by an object and is defined to be equal to the apparent magnitude that the object would have if it were placed at a certain distance from Earth, 10 parsecs for stars. A more complex definition of absolute magnitude is used for planets and small Solar System bodies, based on their brightness at one astronomical unit from the observer and the Sun.

The Sun has an apparent magnitude of −27 and Sirius, the brightest visible star in the night sky, is −1.46. Apparent magnitudes can also be assigned to artificial objects in Earth's orbit with the International Space Station (ISS) sometimes reaching a magnitude of −6.

You can find the brightness of a star in each constellation list on Wikipedia.

Generally, the brightest star in a constellation is nomenclature by α & most of the stars are named in Greek letters.

Here is a list of 1st 49 Brightest Stars. Stars who have an Apparent Brightness of -1 to +1 are called 1st Magnitude Stars.

Rank	App. Brightness	Name of the Star	Bayer Designation	Constellations
1	−1.46	Sirius	α	CMa
2	−0.74	Canopus	α	Car
3	−0.27 (0.01 + 1.33)	Rigil Kentaurus & Toliman	α	Cen
4	−0.05	Arcturus	α	Boo
5	0.03 (−0.02–0.07var)	Vega	α	Lyr
6	0.08 (0.03–0.16var)	Capella	α	Aur
7	0.13 (0.05–0.18var)	Rigel	β	Ori
8	0.34	Procyon	α	CMi
9	0.46 (0.40–0.46var)	Achernar	α	Eri
10	0.50 (0.2–1.2var)	Betelgeuse	α	Ori
11	0.61	Hadar	β	Cen
12	0.76	Altair	α	Aql
13	0.76 (1.33 + 1.73)	Acrux	α	Cru
14	0.86 (0.75–0.95var)	Aldebaran	α	Tau
15	0.96 (0.6–1.6var)	Antares	α	Sco
16	0.97 (0.97–1.04var)	Spica	α	Vir
17	1.14	Pollux	β	Gem
18	1.16	Fomalhaut	α	PsA
19	1.25 (1.21–1.29var)	Deneb	α	Cyg
20	1.25 (1.23–1.31var)	Mimosa	β	Cru
21	1.39	Regulus	α	Leo
22	1.5	Adhara	ε	CMa
23	1.62	Shaula	λ	Sco
24	1.62 (1.98 + 2.97)	Castor	α	Gem
25	1.64	Gacrux	γ	Cru
26	1.64	Bellatrix	γ	Ori
27	1.65	Elnath	β	Tau
28	1.69	Miaplacidus	β	Car
29	1.69 (1.64–1.74var)	Alnilam	ε	Ori
30	1.72 (1.81–1.87var + 4.27)	Regor[a]	γ1,2	Vel

31	1.74	Alnair	α	Gru
32	1.77	Alioth	ε	UMa
33	1.77	Alnitak	ζ	Ori A
34	1.79	Dubhe	α	UMa
35	1.8	Mirfak	α	Per
36	1.82	Wezen	δ	CMa
37	1.84	Sargas	θ	Sco
38	1.85	Kaus Australis	ε	Sgr
39	1.86	Avior	ε	Car
40	1.86	Alkaid	η	UMa
41	1.90 (1.89-1.94var)	Menkalinan	β	Aur
42	1.91	Atria	α	TrA
43	1.92	Alhena	γ	Gem
44	1.94	Peacock	α	Pav
45	1.96 (1.99-2.39var + 5.57)	Alsephina	δ	Vel
46	1.98	Mirzam	β	CMa
47	2	Alphard	α	Hya
48	1.98 (1.86-2.13var)	Polaris	α	UMi
49	2	Hamal	α	Ari

The following four are the most recognizable 1st Magnitude Stars:

1. **Sirius** is the brightest star in the Northern Hemisphere, You can find it in the constellation Canis Major. It is most prominent in the sky during February.

2. **Arcturus** is the brightest star in the constellation Bootes. The color of the Star is red. It is most prominent in the sky during June.

3. **Rigel & Betelgeuse** both belong to the Constellation Orion. Betelgeuse denotes the Right shoulder of Orion whereas Rigel is the star in the left Toe of Orion. It is most prominent in the sky during January.

4. **Vega** is the brightest star in the constellation Lyra. Though Lyra is a small constellation, still Vega looms large. It is the most prominent in the sky during August.

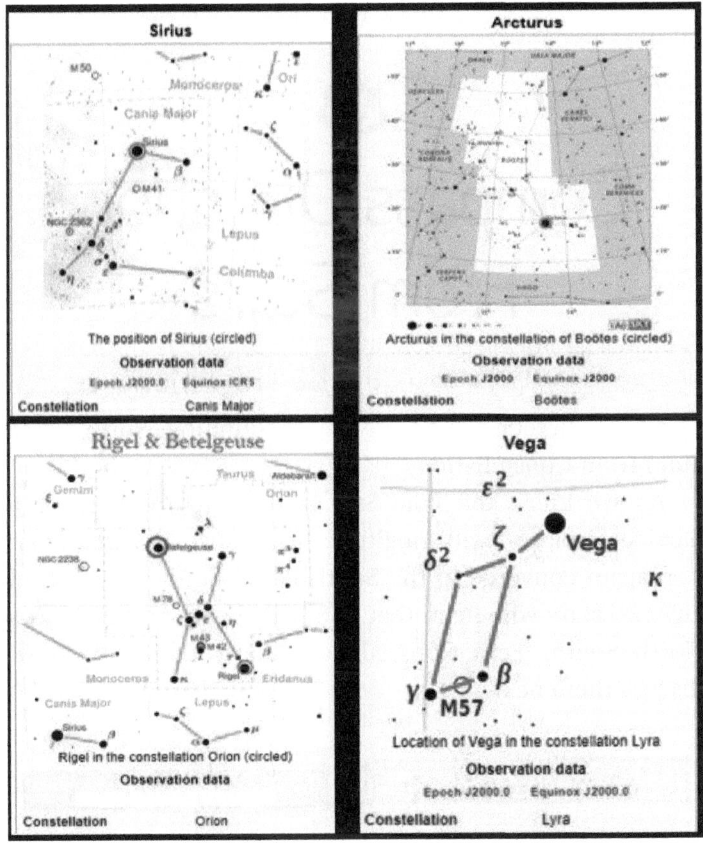
Sirius
M50
Monoceros
Ori
Canis Major
Sirius
OM41
NGC 2362
Lepus
Columba
The position of Sirius (circled)
Observation data
Epoch J2000.0 Equinox ICRS
Constellation Canis Major
Arcturus
Arcturus in the constellation of Boötes (circled)
Observation data
Epoch J2000 Equinox J2000
Constellation Boötes
Rigel & Betelgeuse
Taurus
Aldebaran
Gemini
Orion
NGC 2238
Betelgeuse
M78
M43
M42
Rigel
Monoceros
Eridanus
Canis Major
Lepus
Sirius
Rigel in the constellation Orion (circled)
Observation data
Constellation Orion
Vega
Vega
M57
Location of Vega in the constellation Lyra
Observation data
Epoch J2000.0 Equinox J2000.0
Constellation Lyra

CHAPTER TEN

Compass Direction From Stars

Compass direction generally means finding North (Pole Star) from Constellations.

As we know the Pole Star is fixed in the sky for a particular place & all longitude lines have diverged from it & again converge to the South Point. So, if we can find any two stars who lie in that line will always point towards North/South. Few Constellations have them. We will discuss them next.

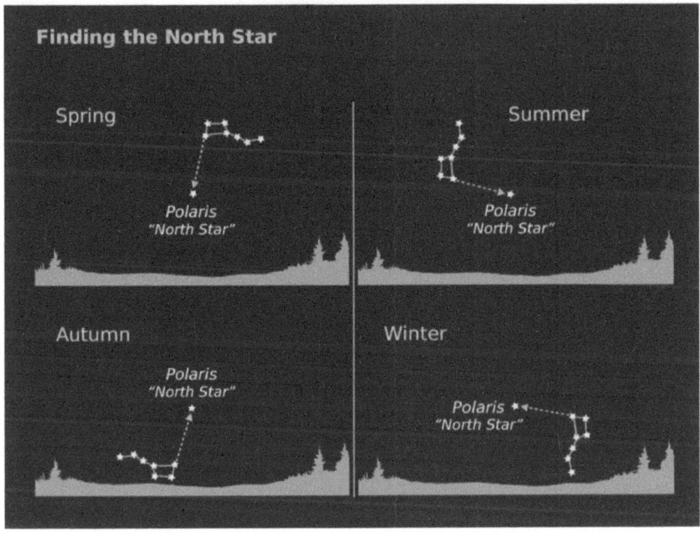

The Big Dipper (US, Canada) or the **Plough** (UK, Ireland) or **Saptarshi** (India) is a large asterism consisting of seven bright stars of the constellation Ursa Major, six of them of the second magnitude, and one, Megrez (δ), of the third magnitude. Four define a "bowl" or "body" and three define a "handle" or "head". It is recognized as a distinct grouping in many cultures. The North Star (Polaris), the current northern pole star, and the tip of the handle of the Little Dipper (Little Bear), can be located by extending an imaginary line through the front two stars of the asterism, Merak (β) and Dubhe (α).
This makes it useful in celestial navigation.

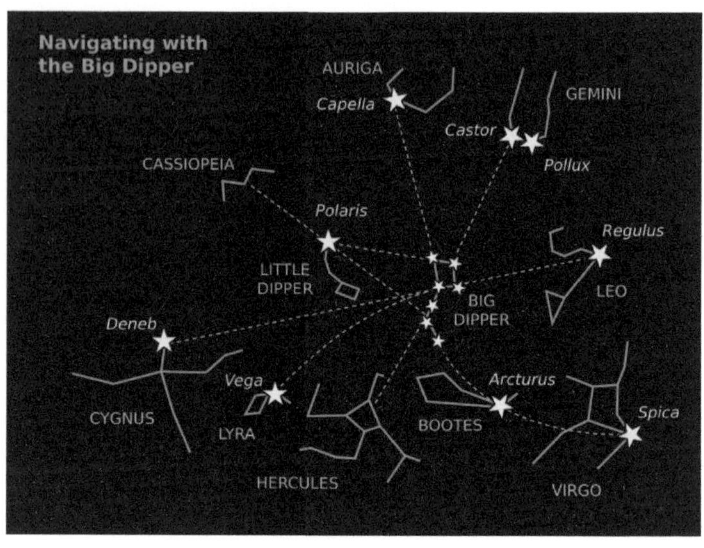
Navigating with the Big Dipper
AURIGA
Capella
GEMINI
Castor
Pollux
CASSIOPEIA
Polaris
Regulus
LITTLE DIPPER
LEO
BIG DIPPER
Deneb
Vega
Arcturus
CYGNUS
LYRA
BOOTES
Spica
HERCULES
VIRGO

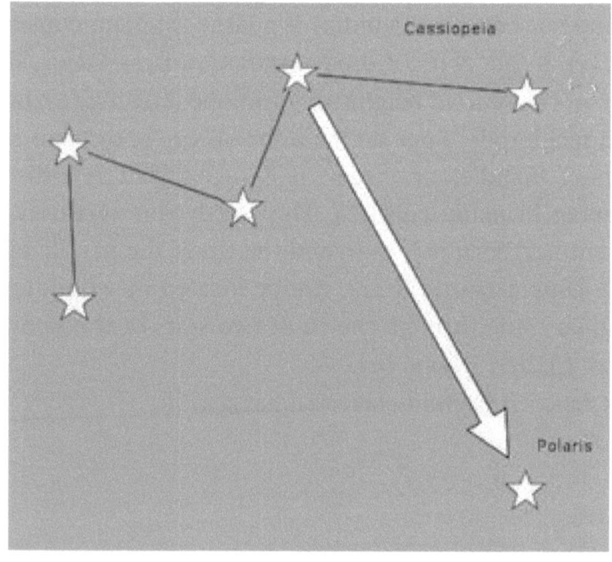
Cassiopeia
Polaris

Cassiopeia can be used lead us to Polaris. In the diagram, can see that Cassiopeia roughly resembles a W or M in the sky, depending on where it is when you locate it. If you draw a line that bisects the first of the two valleys of the W, that line will point toward Polaris, the North Star. Keep in mind that this is not an exact science. It may be off by a few degrees one way or the other, however, it is useful for providing a general direction of travel.

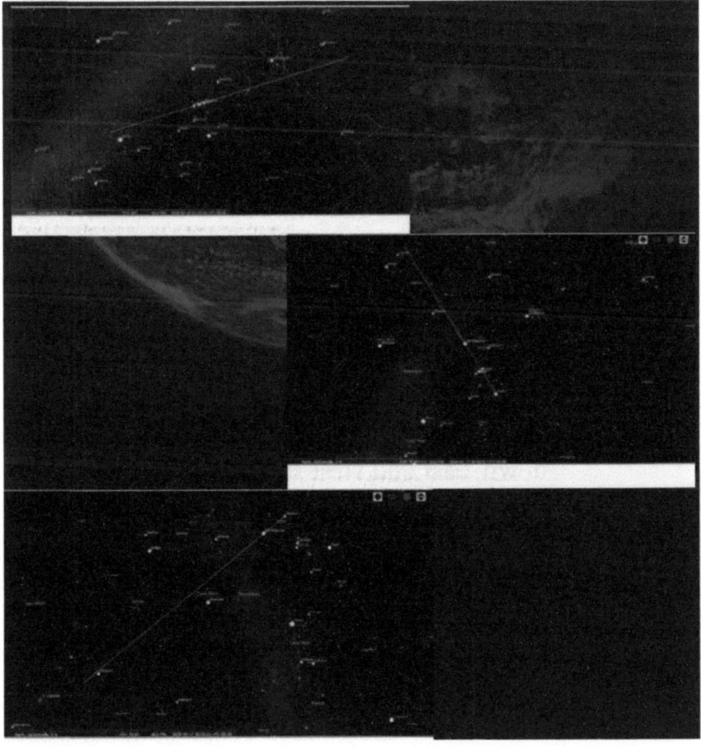

Orion can point us to many other constellations.

If it's still night and you can't find the North Star, there is another way. Find two sticks and lie down. Push one stick into the ground so it's at eye level. Take a second, slightly taller stack and push it into the ground behind the first one, until they line up with a bright star from your position. Watch for five to 10 minutes. If the star moves left you are facing north, right then south, and up and down, east and west respectively.

Sky Map Format

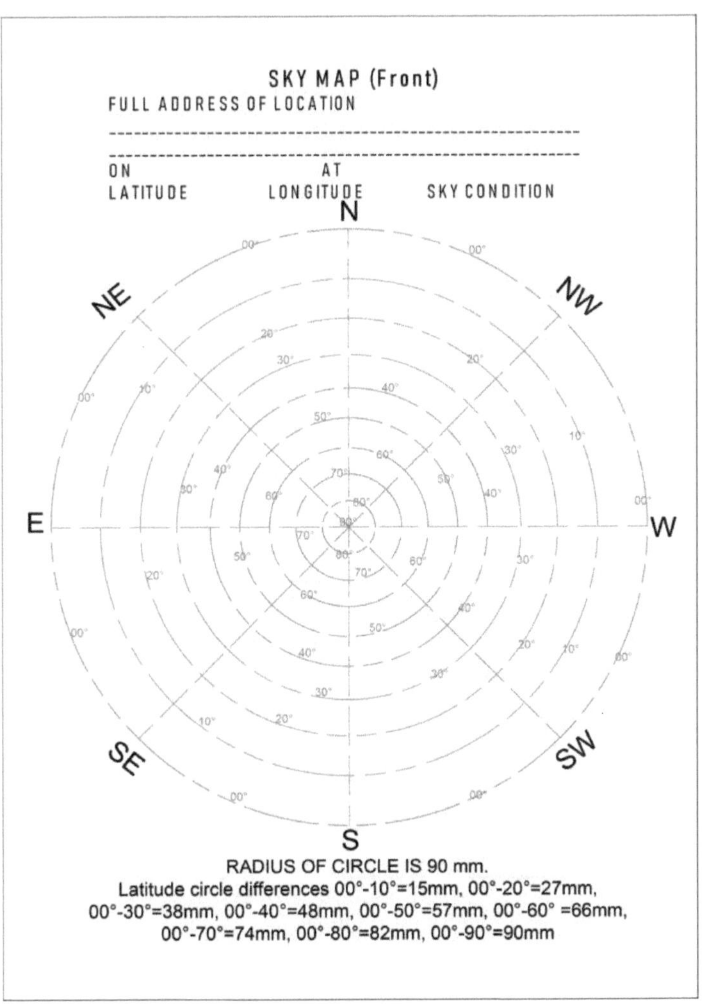

Front Page

SKY MAP FORMAT

SKY MAP (BACK)

Sl No	Object Type (Star/ Planet)	If Identified then write the name	Angle of Object from North at Horizon (NH°)	Angle of the Object from Horizon at Zenith Horizon Line (TH°)	Convert TH° = THp mm as per side table	Conversion Table			
1						5°	8 mm	50°	57 mm
2						10°	15 mm	55°	62 (61.5) mm
3						15°	21 mm	60°	66 mm
4						20°	27 mm	65°	70 mm
5						25°	33 mm	70°	74 mm
6						30°	38 mm	75°	78 mm
7						35°	43 mm	80°	82 mm
8						40°	48 mm	85°	86 mm
9						45°	53 (52.5) mm	90°	90 mm
10									

NAME OF THE SURVEYOR ________________ SIGN ________________

Back Page

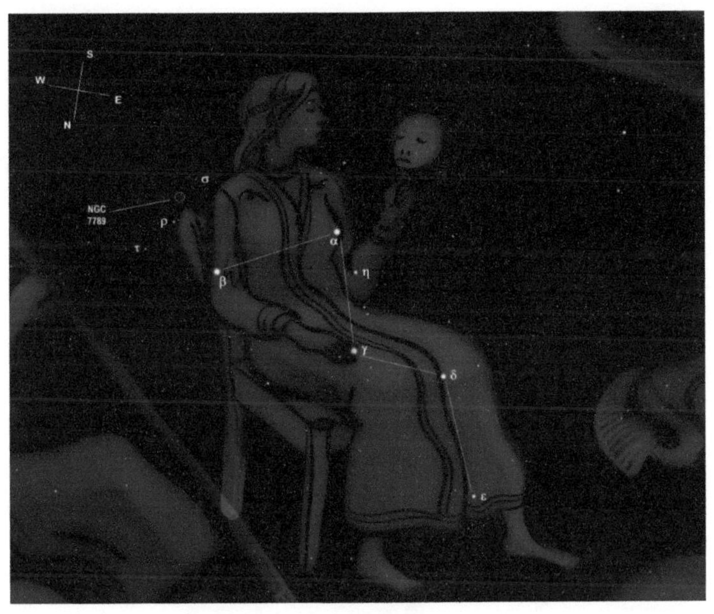

Cassiopeia

CEPHEUS
Pl.4.
GLORIA FREDERICI
LACERTA
CASSIOPEIA
Chaph
CYGNUS
Alderamin
CUSTOS
MESSIUM
Alphirk
Er rai
TARANDUS
DRACO
URSA MINOR
Alruccabah, the Polar Star

Cepheus

BOOTES
CANES VENATICI, COMA BERENICES, AND
Pl.10.
DRACO
HERCULES
CORONA BOREALIS
SERPENS
URSA MAJOR
LEO MINOR
LEO
VIRGO
Arcturus
Mirach
Cor Caroli
Chara
Asterion
Denebola
Vindemiatrix
QUADRANS MURALIS

Bootes

LACERTA, CYGNUS, LYRA, VULPECULA AND ANSER.
CEPHEUS
DRACO

Lyra

Dr. Carl Sagan, 1934-1996

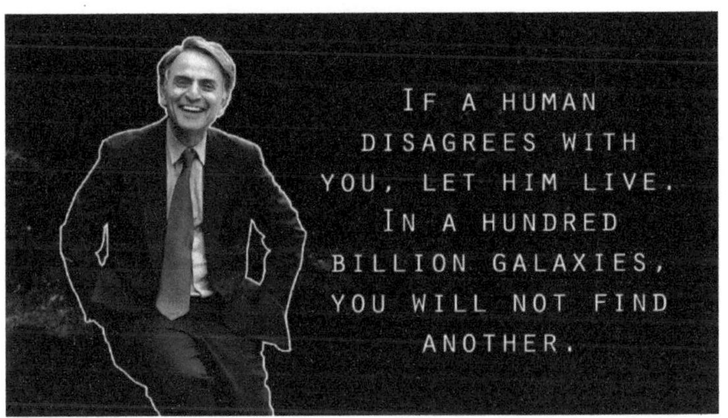

9 798886 848199

Printed by Libri Plureos GmbH in Hamburg,
Germany